AF316806

ADVENTURES OF CARMELO™ SUMMER VACATION

by fred berri

inspired by Carmelo

Published-2023-frederic dalberri
Editor: jc konitz
http://surl.li/jaokl
Illustrations & cover: Faisal Khan

ISBN: 979-8-9855923-8-2

Adventures of Carmelo™
Summer Vacation
by fred berri

DEDICATION
(Italian)

To Carmelo
Ci vediamo quando ci vediamo.

(See you when we see each other)
Love, Poppy

ADVENTURES OF CARMELO™ SUMMER VACATION

by fred berri
inspired by Carmelo

"Well, Carmelo, summer vacation is here and you've finished another year of school. How does it feel to grow so fast? You'll be in the fourth grade next year. Let's look at your chart and see how tall you are now," Daddy said.

"I know, Daddy. I feel like I will be as tall as you are soon. Are we going to take a vacation?" Carmelo asked.

"Wow! Carmelo. You've really grown. Yes, we're going on vacation. We will visit many places and see aunts, uncles, cousins and your grandparents in New York. But we will stop along the way to see interesting sights," Mommy said.

"That sounds exciting. How are we going to go?" Carmelo asked.

"We will drive. We'll stop along the way to see a lots of interesting places that you've learned about in school. Then when we come back from our road trip, we must take a plane to Mexico for Uncle Philip and Aunt Grace's wedding." Mommy said.

"I can't wait to visit those places I learned about in school and I'm excited to see everyone," Carmelo said.

"Yes, it will be fun. Let's go see what you have to pack," Mommy said.

"I'll get the suitcases from the attic," Daddy said.

"What about Jeter?" Carmelo asked, worried the dog would be alone.

"We'll get Merma, the dog sitter to watch him. She will take good care of him," Daddy said.

"Jeter will have fun with Merma. She loves him. He'll have a summer vacation too. I'm ready to go," Carmelo said, laughing.

So, off the family went driving and playing games they could play in the family car. There was plenty of room. Sometimes Mommy would sit with Carmelo in the back while Daddy drove. When they reached Washington, DC, they went sightseeing.

"Wow! There's the White House, where the President and his family live. There's the Capitol and the Lincoln Memorial. President Lincoln's statue is really big. I learned all about this in school.

I'm glad we came to see them in person and not read about them in a book," Carmelo said.

"I can't wait to see our family and I'm happy we are staying at Papa's house. He has chickens. It's fun. He said he will take us to the amusement park," Carmelo said.

Just as Papa promised, they all went to the amusement park and had a fun day on all the rides, eating cotton candy and hot dogs.

"Tomorrow, Carmelo, we're going into New York City to see many landmarks," Mommy said.

The next day, bright and early they ventured into the big city.

"Wow! Look at the Statue of Liberty," Carmelo yelled as the sightseeing boat came close to the Statue.

"It's green," Carmelo said.

"We learned in school that the Statue of Liberty was a gift from France to the United States. It's really big, a lot bigger than it looks in books," Carmelo said.

"That's some big special gift," Mommy and Daddy said.

"The road trip was long but visiting family and all the places we saw was lots of fun.

I have a lot to tell my friends when school starts again," Carmelo said.

"Yes, and now we must go to Mexico for Uncle Philip and Aunt Grace's wedding. We bought you a new suit," Mommy said.

"And we're going on a tour to see an ancient city called 'Tulum' where the Mayan tribe built a castle by the beach thousands of years ago, " Mommy said, showing Carmelo a photo of the castle.

"Wow! That would be cool to live there," Carmelo said.

"This is an exciting and fun summer I'll remember for a long time. Thank you. I can't wait to get home and see Jeter," Carmelo said.

The End!

This is Carmelo

Thank you for reading another story of Carmelo's Adventures.
This is an important part of my journey as an author... having readers. One way to enrich readership and have others enjoy my stories is through reviews. Please help by posting a review at Amazon / Barnes & Noble / Books-A-Million / I-books / Kindle / Nook.

fred berri

Other books in the Adventures of Carmelo™ series

Swim Survival Lesson
The Dentist
The Eye Doctor
Going to the Hospital
Jiu Jitsu
A New Puppy
Adventures of Carmelo™ Coloring Book

COMING SOON...

Moving to a new house in a new neighborhood and a new school in a new state many miles away.

fred berri books are available:

fred berri: https://rb.gy/66wqpv
Amazon: https://rb.gy/e1hsa8
Barnes & Noble: https://rb.gy/bp5fbn

And
ALL ON LINE BOOK RETAIL OUTLETS

* * *

Special Acknowledgements

Carmelo's Parents...Chris & Rachel

About the Author

Mr. Berri graduated Columbia State University. He has volunteered teaching Junior Achievement in the Florida public school district. In addition, he led a volunteer group for a reading program for grades K-3. During his career, he has done public speaking and appeared in a few TV commercials including voice overs. Berri has written many murder mysteries and children's books located:

fredberri.com/Amazon/Barnes & Noble/Books-a-Million/and...
All online Book Sellers

5 Star Award-winning Author

Reader's Favorite 5 Star Award...
Provides professional reviews for authors and has earned the respect of renowned publishers such as Random House, Simon & Schuster and Harper Collins. Readers' Favorite also tries to help those in need by donating books and income each year to St. Jude Children's Research Hospital.

Donate: ***http://surl.li/ixfpq***

Firebird Book 5 Star Award...

Firebird Book Awards are sponsored by Speak Up Talk Radio that advocates Enchanted Makeovers which renovates and transforms long term shelters for women and children into places of peace and possibility. Enchanted Makeovers have impacted over 60, 000 people nationally.

You can donate and help women and children. Visit to find out more & Donate: https://enchantedmakeovers.org/programs-projects/